I Only Want to Help and Heal

BRUNO GRÖNING

I Only Want to Help and Heal

THE LIFE OF BRUNO GRÖNING
For children, young people and adults

Thomas Eich

Grete Häusler GmbH

© 2006 by Grete Häusler GmbH - Verlag
Rheindahlener Straße 78
41189 Mönchengladbach, Germany
Tel. +49 2166 9599-0 • Fax. +49 2166 9599-59
E-mail: info@gh-verlag.de • Internet: www.gh-verlag.de

Internet: bruno-groening.org/english

1st Edition 2007

ISBN 978-3-933344-92-2 englisch

Original edition in German:
Bruno Gröning - Ich will nur helfen und heilen
ISBN 978-3-933344-54-0 deutsch

CONTENTS

Glossary of German words:

Heilstrom: This is what Bruno Gröning called the spiritual force that causes healing. He also used the terms "healing wave" and "divine force" synonymously.

Einstellen: A person "tunes in" to the divine force and absorbs it.

Regelungen: The streaming in of the force starts a cleansing process in the body that can also express itself as pain. The illness is cleansed out of the body. Bruno Gröning called this Regelung.

Foreword

Dear readers,

As you are now holding a book about Bruno Gröning in your hands, you must expect nothing but the truth, the truth about and around Bruno Gröning. This truth is of the greatest possible value for the life of all human beings. Truth is what everyone needs for their life here on earth. Truth will win out and become reality.

This book about Bruno Gröning shows you what this little man from Danzig experienced and suffered, what he did, and who persecuted him.

Even after he was grown up, Bruno Gröning said of himself: "I am only a child." Just as children nowadays have a tough time in the hard world of adults, he had the same experience, but all through his life. He refused to take into himself the world's hard-heartedness. He fought that people might keep sympathy and love of their neighbour alive within them and preserve what is heavenly and divine in themselves. He kept it within himself. He would not let it be taken from him. He also fought so that whoever had already lost it should have the chance to regain it.

In order to get there he had to clear the path again, the path that was blocked with thorny bushes – the divine path. The connection to God had been cut and he had to rebuild this connection. He had to reconstruct the bridge back to God for all human beings. He had to lead them from their path of suffering back to the divine path. That was not easy. It stirred up many opposing forces that did everything possible to destroy him.

But Bruno Gröning didn't let that get him down. He went on his way, so clearing the path for everyone, the path to health, joy, bliss and confidence.

If you, dear readers, read this book carefully, follow the life story of Bruno Gröning attentively, and take his life into your hearts, you will understand why Bruno Gröning had to come. You will see why it was necessary that someone had to come again to bring what is good and divine to humankind, to awaken faith in them, bringing them the strength to believe. Someone to recreate their connection to God, and take them back to love, peace and joy.

I wish that you may experience all the good Bruno Gröning had to give and still has to give to this day. But you must keep a sharp lookout so that you also spot all the evil that Bruno Gröning opposed. Reject it, and take in everything that is divine as it reveals itself in the works of Bruno Gröning. May truth and clarity shine in you. I wish you all the best!

Thomas Eich

AS AN INTRODUCTION

"I am and remain a child, I shall not change myself, no, and all of you and everyone can believe what you will. I am and remain a child, am only a child of God, no more. I am not proud, no, nor [too] cowardly to say so, because I know I am only a child. But many people are not children any more, because they are grown up."

Bruno Gröning

1. CHILDHOOD AND YOUTH

Bruno Gröning was born in Danzig on May 30, 1906. Danzig is a city in the far east of Europe. It lies by the Baltic Sea and is surrounded by great forests. Today Danzig belongs to Poland and is called Gdansk, but at that time it still belonged to Germany.

When Bruno was born, his parents already had three children. Three more were born after him. So he was the fourth of seven children, right in the middle.

Bruno Gröning (3rd from left) among his brothers and sisters

His parents were simple people. His father August was a bricklayer foreman, and his mother Margarethe came fror a family of tradesmen.

Even while Bruno was very small, his parents noticed he was different from their other children. Sometime' his father came home shouting and cursing, loud voi heard coming from little Bruno's room. When the frightened parents went to check, everything was calm again and the child lay peacefully in his crib. But the father would stop shouting and walk quietly around the house.

Experiences like this alienated both his parents, and his brothers and sisters as well. His father even found it spooky. The more Bruno grew, the stranger he became to the others. He was soon considered unusual and was often called a "weirdo".

An Unusual Experience

Repelled by the hard-heartedness of his surroundings, little Bruno often fled to nature. He felt more attracted to animals, trees and bushes than to people. He often disappeared for days into the nearby woods. He once wrote about it, stating:

"Here I experienced God. In every bush, in every tree, in every animal. Yes, even in the rocks. I could stand everywhere for hours – there really was no concept of time – reflecting, and I always felt inside as though my whole inner life was widening out into infinity."

His parents had no sympathy for their son's escapades. When he was found and brought home after days in the woods, he was whipped and beaten black and blue.

At some point he could no longer stand being at home. Again he ran into the woods and prayed to God. He no longer wanted to remain here on earth and said:

"God, why did you send me here? I don't want to remain here, I sense only evil here. That cannot be. I do not want to be here."

God, his Father, answered him:

As he grew up, Bruno Gröning kept
his great love of plants and animals.

"You have seen the need, misery and pain of human beings and wanted to help them. You begged me to be permitted to come down to earth to free them of that and I allowed
you to do so, and now you are here!"

Little Bruno - he was just two and a half years old - understood why he was alive on earth and what his task here was.
Then the thought came to him:

"Aren't people your friends too? So why do I always run
away from people? Animals fear the evil in people, but I am
not afraid, because I am stronger than evil. I want to show
everybody that I am stronger."

"You really aren't sick any more."

What he meant when he said: "I am stronger than evil" soon became clear. Animals and people became healthy in his presence. He once described how it came about:

"Another thought came to me as I was standing before a sick human body: the sickness vanished from the bodies of some animals when I softly whispered, 'Dear little animal, you will soon have a healthy body again', and that was what happened. It is really no different for people. As the thought remained firm within me, the body of that person became free of all complaints. So I was always attracted directly to the sick, because in all the houses where I suddenly showed up, there were some sick people. I always simply said to them, 'You really aren't sick any more.' If some of them said that someone was dying, I said briefly, 'No, he won't die for a long time yet. He'll be healthy.'

"I was with each sick person only briefly. I would approach the sick person and quietly and briefly tell him what I have already mentioned above. Then I would disappear quick as lightning each time."

During the First World War he often went to military hospitals. Many soldiers were lying there who had been wounded in the war.

Little Bruno was soon a welcome guest there. The wounded felt well in his presence and many became well again.

In his autobiographical notes Bruno Gröning wrote about that time:

"During my childhood and youth which I spent in my parent's house, I became more and more aware of strange abilities which – radiating from me – had a calming and healing influence upon people and animals.

"Already as a small child, sick people became free of their ailments in my presence and children as well as adults who were quarrelling or upset became totally calm with a few quiet words from me. As a child I also noticed that animals that were supposed to be shy or fierce were gentle and tame with me. My situation at home was therefore unusual and tense. I soon tried hard to become fully independent, in order to get away from the environment of being misunderstood by my family,"

Subject to God

When he was nine years old Bruno got sick. He got dysentery, a severe intestinal disease from which many people died in those days. He lost a lot of weight and lay in a fever for weeks. His parents were in despair and the doctor did not know what to do. He could not help the boy. Everybody thought that he was going to die. Later he said about that time:

"For a whole year I slept on the bare ground without one piece of clothing, thirsty and hungry. My body was just skin and bones! I refused every doctor and every human help and just subjected myself to the will of God, our Lord. And when I got up a year later, my body was healthy again."

Now he had experienced it himself. He had experienced in his own body that God can still help when people can no longer help. He thus could say with full conviction later:

"There is nothing incurable! God is the greatest physician!"

School and Apprenticeship Years

Bruno never joined the many wild fights of his brothers and sisters and children of the neighbourhood. But the children often made fun of him. Sometimes they even hit him because he was so different. One of his brothers once even broke his nose. But he never hit back.

Bruno Gröning (2ⁿᵈ from right) working on a construction site

He attended school for a total of six years. Elementary school normally lasted that long then. However, he had missed a whole year of school because of the dysentery.

After his school days he did a commercial apprenticeship. But two years later, at the urging of his father, he gave it up. As a bricklayer foreman, he wanted his son to learn a building trade too, and had him trained as a carpenter. But Bruno

Gröning did not finish that either. Three months before the end of his training, the company went out of business. In the difficult times following the war, there weren't enough contracts. Bruno Gröning found himself on the street without a diploma.

In the years that followed, Bruno Gröning worked at all sorts of jobs. He made himself independent with a company for construction and furniture-making. He worked at the harbour, in the post office, at a chocolate factory and as an electrician (low voltage installation). He once said about that time:

"In particular I wanted to do practical work through which I could study people's knowledge and know-how in all situations in life and at all levels of society and understand how people shaped their lives. I didn't just look for the poorest of the poor, but also for the richest of the rich to find out how they lived. A private life, as it is understood in the usual sense (movies, pubs, card games, etc.) did not interest me."

2. THE TIME IN DANZIG AND THE WAR

He married when he was 21 years old. But his wife had no understanding for him. She just wanted him for herself and wrote off the healings as weird, just nonsense or strange moods).

In 1931 and 1939 his sons Harald and Günter were born. They were his great joy, but they both died young. Although many people had already become healthy through Bruno

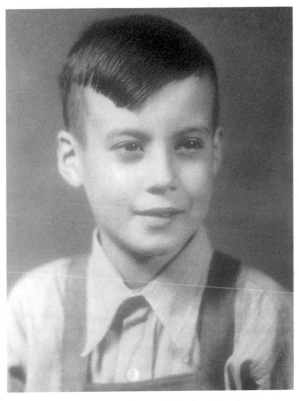

Bruno Gröning's second son, Günther

Gröning, his wife did not believe in her husband's healing power. When the children fell ill, she kept them away from him and put them both into hospital behind his back. But the doctors could not help. Harald died while still in Danzig and Günter later in Dillenburg. They both only lived to the age of nine. Those were hard blows of fate for Bruno Gröning. Years later he still shed tears when he spoke about his sons.

The time between the two world wars was a time of preparation for his later work. He endured bitter experiences in order to understand people in every life situation better and learn to sympathize with their distress.

More Healings

Many healings happened at that time as well. His father later wrote:

"I myself was suffering from a severe ailment, so that the doctors had given me up already. A brief treatment* from my son Bruno was enough to make me completely healthy again."

A neighbour explained:

"I already experienced Bruno Gröning's healing power during the years as his neighbour in Danzig-Langfuhr. I was often relieved of pain."

Another neighbour reported:

"From 1928 I knew Mr. Gröning in Danzig, which is my home town. Mr. Gröning was already interested in spiritual things at that time and he helped and healed people. I know

---

* Bruno Gröning did not treat illnesses. But his father did not know any other expression to describe his son's effect.

of about twenty cases that were successful. (…) I can also furnish many proofs where Mr. Gröning helped children, for example, who were paralyzed or could not hear or see. It worked in every case. We ourselves, as well as the people whom he helped, are still facing an enigma. We used to rack our brains, wondering how such a thing could be."

Another neighbour later wrote an extensive report about that time. He relates among other things:

"Very often he gave up his sleep or money. There was only one thing that mattered for him: helping. In those days he was often called to see some sick people who begged him for help, yes, even at night. But he never took a single penny for it, no matter who it was. On the contrary, he would often give even the last money he had to those people. When someone thanked him for some deed, Bruno Gröning would refuse their thanks. He told them that they should express their gratitude by doing something good for another fellow human being. I was allowed to be his companion in many cases and convince myself of what he did."

War Time

In 1939 the Second World War began. That was a truly horrible event. It was a war that spread across almost the whole earth, in which many millions of people were killed. In 1943 Bruno Gröning had to become a soldier. But he had some problems during his time in the army. He had said:

"Whether you send me to the front or not, I simply won't shoot anybody. I can't do that."

For this reason they wanted to court-martial him. He could have been sentenced to death there. But in the end he

Bruno Gröning also had to become a soldier

was sent to the front anyway, where enemy soldiers met and fought one another.

But even then Bruno Gröning's main wish was to help others. Even at the front he used every opportunity to work for his mates or for the people.

In one Russian village for instance, he gained access to army food supplies for people on the verge of death through starvation. During his time as a prisoner of war in Russia he later organized better clothing for his comrades, better food and better quarters. He helped to heal countless people suffering from starvation oedema, with very swollen, fat bellies. In the horror of war he never killed anyone, but helped many people.

Leaving the Homeland

When the war was over, Bruno Gröning returned from captivity at the end of 1945. But Danzig was occupied. He could no longer remain there. So he came to Dillenburg. He built himself a new life and brought his family there. But after his second son had died and his wife wanted to forbid him from doing any helping activities, he separated from her. He felt it was his duty to share the healing powers that he possessed with all people. He said:

"I don't belong to individuals, I belong to humanity."

At the beginning of 1949 his path led him to the Ruhr district. Due to reports by a few people who had been healed, more and more people became aware of him. He moved from house to house, wherever he was needed, wherever sick people asked for help. He worked like this in small circles until March 1949. Then an engineer invited him to the town of Herford to visit his sick son.

3. DRAGGED INTO THE PUBLIC EYE

Dieter Hülsmann was nine years old. He suffered from muscular distrophy and was immobile, lying in bed for several weeks. His parents had taken him to see several doctors and professors but none of them were able to help him.

Bruno Gröning with Dieter Hülsmann and his parents

On March 15 Bruno Gröning visited the Hülsmann family and spoke to the boy. Afterwards the child was able to get up, walk and even climb stairs. His parents were overjoyed and the father talked about his son's healing everywhere. That's how Bruno Gröning became known in Herford.

Day by day more people seeking healing arrived. More and more people heard about the mysterious event. Further healings occurred. Before long Gröning's name was on everyone's lips. The newspapers called him the "miracle doctor." Very soon people all over Germany were talking about the strange man who could simply make illnesses disappear. Thousands of seekers of help streamed into Herford. Crowds of people camped around the Hülsmann house in Wilhelmsplatz.

Onslaught of the huge crowds around Bruno Gröning

All Humanity's Misery

In a brochure from that time, A. Kaul, a doctor of philosophy, gave an impressive description of the situation in front of the Hülsmann house:

"In their thousands the diseased and the infirm are coming into the little Westphalian town that harbours the miracle doctor within its walls. By bus, truck, car, by train and on foot, in horse-drawn carts and on bicycles, in little hand-drawn wagons, in wheelchairs and by ambulance, day and night, crowds of people are arriving. They are coming to the Wilhelmsplatz in Herford, which lies in the shadow of the Protestant church. There, at house number 7, Bruno

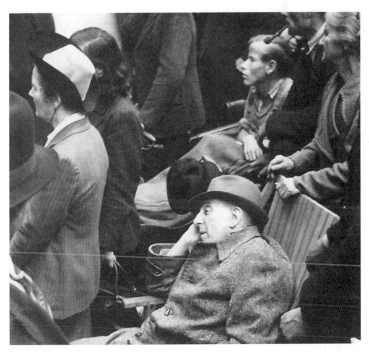

An image of sorrow

Gröning has found lodging with the parents of a child whom he healed. The human misery to be seen here is shattering and endless. In the surrounding gardens and parks, on deck chairs or stretchers, the sick are waiting day and night for healing. During the night of June 17 the police wanted to put up some fifty mothers with very small children in barracks. But no words of friendly persuasion could get them to leave the spot, not even when it started to rain. They streamed together from all regions of Germany, the hopeless and the afflicted, the young and the old, men, women, girls, children, from all walks of life and all levels of society. There were Americans, English, Belgians, Swiss, Swedes, Hungarians, Poles. There were even Romanies, who gathered here in crowds after the successful healing of a dumb Romany child. The lame came, the blind, the deaf, a whole community of misery and poverty. These people are wretched, whether they are sitting in luxury cars or painfully moving on their crutches. The hopeless and the hopeful, the tired and despairing, hundreds and thousands of them, but they all have just one wish: to find healing! None of them asks whether the events here have a stamp of official approval from some office or ministry, or whether science is for it or against it, or whether the one who is to heal them is a messiah or an educated man. They simply want to be healed of their pain. They want to become happy, active people again. They want to become healthy again."

Bruno Gröning on the Balcony

Bruno Gröning did not remain in Herford all the time. He was often on his way to other towns and villages to see people who had asked him for help. Those seeking healing in Herford sometimes spent days waiting for him. And the numbers increased to hundreds and thousands.

On his return the waiting crowds stormed him. A journalist once described it this way:

"7:40 p.m.: Gröning arrives. The crowds press against him, trying to take his hand, or at least to touch his clothes. He has a hard time getting into the corridor. (…)

"11 p.m.: Gröning steps out onto the balcony. The crowd has now grown to 600 or 700 people. The people below gaze at his face, as if mesmerized. Gröning calmly finishes smoking his cigarette. Then he begins to speak, in a clear way, but without too much emotion:

"'My dear seekers of healing! Your pleas and prayers to the Lord God were not in vain. For today the town authorities have exceptionally given me permission to heal. I make you aware that healing only benefits those who carry in themselves faith in our Lord God, or are prepared to take faith in. I herewith declare you all healthy in the name of God. I point out to you that one or the other of you still feels slight pain. Those are Regelungen* pains that will disappear very soon, if you go on firmly having faith in the healing.

"'I also know that many people in other places have become healthy at this moment. Whoever has come here on behalf of a sick relative can go home comforted. Healing also happens without my presence. The goal of my wishes is to help all people back to health. I don't ask about their religion. I don't ask about their nationality.'

"After a few seconds' pause he continued: 'I ask you now: Who is still feeling pain?' About 20 people raise their hands. Gröning's eyes run through the crowd. Then he says, 'Who still has pain now?' A young man raises his hand. Gröning

---

* **Regelungen:** see glossary of German words on page 6

says, 'That is not the original pain! No. Don't worry. I have spoken to you. The point where you are suffering is already affected by the healing.'

"In the meantime a murmur ripples through the crowd. People are twisting and stretching. 'I'm really healthy! Thank God!', or 'My leg is slowly loosening up', or 'I can see again!' I hear shouts like this coming up from the crowd. But very few people are talking otherwise. That amazes me.

Bruno Gröning continues, 'I ask you now not to grumble, because whoever doubts their healing, doubts our Lord, God.

Bruno Gröning speaking
from the balcony to the crowds

I ask you not to direct your thanks for this healing to me. Thanks are due to our Lord God alone. I don't ask anyone for a reward. But I do expect you to pray to God all your life. Life without God is no life. A human being is only worthy of being spoken to as such if he has faith in the Lord God.'"

The Miracle of Herford

But Bruno Gröning didn't just speak to people from the balcony. He also took care of individual people and dealt with the poorest of the poor. In a brochure of that time we find the following passage:

"Among the seekers of healing who are waiting at 7 Wilhelmsplatz there are also some English men and women who have heard about Gröning's fame. One German doctor appeared promptly with three of his patients. First, a young man with TB of the lungs and bones and with a stiffened left leg, second, a boy paralyzed in both legs, and third, a young girl with chronic nervous headaches.

"Gröning does not do any diagnoses. Speaking directly to the young man with TB, he tells him to pay particular attention to the bones in his left leg. 'What do you feel now?'

Bruno Gröning taking care of the poorest of the poor

'A hot stream is flowing through my body.' 'And now?' 'It's tingling in my left leg.' 'Now lift your leg as high as I am doing, now!' Gröning shows him how, lifting his own leg up to his abdomen. The young man hesitates. 'You can do it just as well as I can!' Without any visible strain the sick man lifts the leg that had been so stiff into the same position. In disbelief he looks first at his leg, then at his doctor. 'Can it be possible? I can move my leg!' 'You'll get healthy, but it will be slow for you. Write to me!' And to the doctor: 'Keep me informed!'

"The boy paralyzed in both legs is sitting next to his mother with his two crutches: 'My boy, get up!' The mother interrupts, 'He can't get up, he is lame!' Gröning turns his head. 'You should not say that!' he tells her, almost severely. 'You are holding on to your child's illness! My boy, get up, you can do it!' Red spots appear on the child's thin face, his mouth trembles and tears roll from his eyes. The many people standing in the room are moved. They watch as the boy rises from the armchair, standing there, alone, without his crutches. 'And now, come to me!' With unsteady steps he walks towards Gröning who takes him by the hand, looking into his eyes for a long time. Lovingly he strokes the head of the child and sends him back to his mother: 'Keep exercising slowly. Don't demand too much. The legs are still too weak. Use the crutches once more going home, but you'll soon be able to throw them away!' A child's happy eyes and a happy mother are his thanks.

"The young girl with the chronic headaches is already healed before Gröning addresses her. No, she has no more pain. 'Do you want the pain back?' 'No, no, for God's sake, no!' comes the reply from her lips.

"What about the doctor? He had been watching speechlessly. He offers Gröning his hand, saying, 'Mr. Gröning, I am totally at your disposal. I am committing myself to you!'"

Healing upon Healing

In June 1949 a reporter described the conditions in Herford this way: "It was an indescribable picture of misery. There were innumerable lame people in wheel chairs, others who were carried by their relatives, blind people, deaf mutes, mothers with retarded and lame children, little old women and young men, all of them groaning and pressing together in front of the house. Almost a hundred cars, trucks and buses were parked in the square and they all came from far away.

"'Do you believe that you will be healed?' I asked the sick. They nodded. 'You should have been here yesterday,' one of them replied to me. Mr. Gröning was in Viersen in the Rhineland and five paralyzed people stood up here in the courtyard and went home healthy. Healing at a distance: just being in the yard made them healthy.' The other sick people confirmed it.

"I pressed on through the crowd and took down their mysterious tales in shorthand. There were enough to fill a book. As I lit a cigarette, a young man next to me asked me: 'Please, sell me one!' He wore a uniform jacket and looked like a POW, home from Russia. So I gave him a cigarette. He lit it and full of high spirits said, 'You see, I can do everything myself now.' He moved his right arm as well as his fingers and his right leg. 'Have you been healed by Gröning too?' I asked him. 'Yes I was paralyzed on my right side in Russia. Mr. Gröning looked at me and now I am totally healthy again. I still can't grasp it.' Happily he swung his arms and legs around.

"I steered toward a group milling around a white-haired woman of around forty years. 'Of course,' I heard the woman say, 'I have been healed through Mr. Gröning. I had huge gastric ulcers, kept losing weight and could no longer sleep for all the pain. Twelve of us came to Gröning. (…) He looked at me and I felt as though the ulcers were falling to the ground like a stone. I've had no more pain ever since. I keep putting on weight, and the X-rays I had taken showed clearly that the ulcers have disappeared. I went to the Medical Examination Committee and I can tell you, were they ever amazed!' The woman went on, 'But that's nothing yet! Last week a blind man stood here in the courtyard. He waited several days and nights. As I frequently come here, I noticed him. I felt sorry for him and I invited him to come and eat. 'No,' he declined, 'I must not miss the moment when Mr. Gröning comes out.' So I brought him some rolls and told him that I would make sure that he would be taken to the train station. 'I don't need anybody, because I'll be able to go to the station by myself.' And then I experienced it with my own eyes. Mr. Gröning came and the young man cried out, 'I can see again!' Indeed, the veil had been removed from his eyes. He described the handbag I was carrying in my hand. He said, 'There is a car driving over there and that is the number plate,' and he did indeed find his way to the station alone. Everybody standing around him cried with joy."

The Healing Ban

More and more healings occurred. More and more people came. So it did not take long before the authorities became alert to the strange happenings on the Wilhelmsplatz. Some influential doctors took it upon themselves to ask the town council to put an end to the activities around the "miracle doctor." They were Bruno Gröning's declared enemies and did everything they could to limit his activity. On May 3, 1949, on their insistence, the town of Herford issued Bruno Gröning with a healing ban.

In Germany there is a law regulating complementary health practitioners and this law determines who may heal and who may not heal. Bruno Gröning was accused of having broken this law because he was really not permitted to heal at all.

An investigation committee was formed. Bruno Gröning was asked to demonstrate his healing abilities in a scientific examination. But their intentions were not honest. Some time later, when a certain Professor Fischer was looking for a hospital in which Bruno Gröning could be "clinically tested", he checked a hospital in Bielefeld. The manager there was a member of the Herford investigation committee and during Professor Fischer's visit all the members of the committee were present. Bruno Gröning was supposed to prove his ability on some of the patients in the hospital. But when Professor Fischer asked to see these sick people, he realized that almost without exception each one of them was on the verge of dying. Their will to live was already snuffed out. It was a trap, and Bruno Gröning was supposed to fall into it.

One of the doctors there made no bones about the fact that it was his aim to "shoot" Bruno Gröning down. Another one said, "Gröning can prove what he likes, but he won't receive a permit to heal."

Yet another declared,

"Dealing with Bruno Gröning goes against the honour of the medical profession."

Thus, right from the start Bruno Gröning had to stand up against some powerful opposing forces. He fought against the healing ban with all his might. He did everything to continue helping the sick who were crowding around him. But it was no use. The healing ban remained in place. By the end of June he had to leave Herford permanently. All his efforts had failed.

The Healing Ban – Bruno Gröning has to leave Herford

4. A SCIENTIFIC EXPERIMENT

At about the same time three employees of the magazine Revue came to Herford, two reporters and the Professor Fischer mentioned in the last chapter. They spoke with healed people and checked their reports. They were surprised by the results and had to admit that some unusual healings had taken place. The magazine Revue decided to finance a scientific investigation of the "Gröning phenomenon" and to report about it exclusively. Professor von Weizsäcker was to investigate the "healing method" of the "miracle doctor", as they called him, at the university clinic in Heidelberg.

Bruno Gröning accepted the offer. A positive report was promised him if the outcome was positive. This was supposed to smooth the way towards his freedom to practise.

On July 27, 1949, the examinations began. Bruno Gröning was to prove his abilities on people who were chosen from among the patients at the university clinic, and also from over 80 000 letters of petition that had been brought from Herford to Heidelberg. Every person chosen was carefully examined. Then they were brought to Gröning and he was to show what he could do. The doctors were always there and observed carefully all that took place. They wanted to know what he was doing and how he was doing it. The results impressed them most profoundly.

Healings under Doctors' Scrutiny

The doctors became witnesses of how illnesses which they themselves were unable to heal simply vanished. They were especially impressed by the healings of patients from their own clinic, some of whom they had already known for years.

There was Else Jost, for instance. She was 36 years old and had suffered from a severe intestinal disease for thirteen years. She had chronic constipation, a lot of pain and sometimes she could not go to the toilet for a week. She had been unsuccessfully treated at the Heidelberg clinic for quite some time. After Bruno Gröning dealt with her, she became healthy. A follow-up checkup at the clinic confirmed it. The doctors were up against an enigma.

Another case was that of Mr. Strobel. He suffered from ankylosing spondilitis. His spine was completely rigid. He could not move his head any more and had considerable pain when he walked and climbed stairs. Here again Bruno Gröning spoke with him and the problems vanished. He felt well and his problems when walking were completely removed. He too had a follow-up examination at the clinic and his healing was confirmed.

How Bruno Gröning acted upon the sick and what he said to them was recorded on tape. The magazine Revue reprinted some of it. Here is a small extract of Bruno Gröning's conversation with Mr. Stroebel:

Gröning: Take a few steps!

Strobel: I had pain in the region of my groin, mostly while climbing stairs, just couldn't go up, it hurt a lot, more on the left than the right.

Gröning: Try and climb up the stairs!

Strobel walks to the stairs, suddenly leaps up and down the stairs. He is overjoyed.

Gröning: Turn your head to the right and the left!

Strobel: It grinds as though there was some sand inside.

Gröning: How is it now?

Strobel: It's getting easier for me.

Gröning: Has the grinding stopped?

Strobel: No, it's still grinding!

Gröning: Just hold your hand there....take your hand away!

Strobel is still moving his head.

Gröning: It's getting less.

The Strobel case

Strobel: (Still moving his head). Yes, it is working well.

Gröning is dealing with other patients.

Strobel: I feel light, I have no more pain, not even in the pelvic bones. All pain is gone.

Gröning asks Strobel to climb the stairs one more time. Strobel leaps easily up and down again.

No Charlatan

Even in Herford the question kept coming up whether Bruno Gröning really could do something or whether he was just a charlatan and a swindler. The tests in Heidelberg were supposed make this clear. The magazine Revue printed what Professor Fischer wrote in a report following the examinations:

"Bruno Gröning is no charlatan, no hypnotizer, no miracle doctor, but a gifted non-medical psychotherapist (physician of the soul). He tries to help people, moved by his childlike nature and sympathy based on religion."

So the question was answered. Bruno Gröning was no charlatan. But Professor Fischer's explanation did not really do justice to the Gröning phenomenon. It tried to explain the events happening around Gröning from a purely psychotherapeutic point of view. But he could not grasp the true nature of Bruno Gröning's work. He did not consider the most important fact, nor did the medical experts in Heidelberg: the fact that Bruno Gröning kept stressing that God was the greatest physician and that really it was He who made the healings happen.

No Collaboration, No Report

The final report about Bruno Gröning was to be written after the evaluation of all the results. He was promised that this would finally free the way for him to go on working.

In the meantime Professor Fischer and the patron of the entire project, Professor Weizsäcker, made Bruno Gröning a proposal. They offered to build a sanatorium where he could work alongside doctors. But they wanted to manage everything and select the patients themselves. Gröning was to have no say in that. In addition, he was also to take on some financial responsibilities.

He once wrote about this offer:

"The financial conditions, etc., that Professor Fischer proposed in this connection were so laid down that they were unacceptable to me. Naturally many discussions took place, also with gentlemen who wanted to finance this work. I could not declare myself in agreement with Professor Fischer's proposals and refused them because:

1. I didn't have a single penny of money, so I could not take over any financial responsibilities to him that I could not have met.
2. I had never thought of making a business of the whole project.

"All of this was, therefore, an impossible demand. Besides, I only wanted to do that which was given to me by my calling: to help those seeking help, and therefore to make myself available to doctors such as psychotherapists, but never to make a business out of the whole thing."

When the deal didn't materialize, the gentlemen professors lost their interest in Bruno Gröning. The promised report was never made. Instead of making it possible for him to work freely, more and more stones were laid in his path. During the examinations his work was described in medical terms. The words "treatment", "patients" and "healing method" had been used, which described Bruno Gröning's work as a medical activity. That was to cause him a lot of damage later.

5. THE TRABERHOF

After closing the Heidelberg experiments, Bruno Gröning turned towards South Germany in August 1949. He wanted to escape the commotion going on around him. The owner of a horse-breeding farm close to Rosenheim invited him to the estate, called the Traberhof. Bruno Gröning wanted to take a calm look at the offers for setting up sanatoriums.

The Traberhof, near Rosenheim

At first they managed to keep his presence there secret. It was wonderfully peaceful on the Traberhof. But rumours soon began to circulate. Gröning was said to be in Bavaria. Journalists set out to look for him. Prize money was offered. Who would find Gröning first? Who would have the first interview with him?

Gröning in Bavaria

It didn't take them long to get on his tracks. The newspapers wrote reports. They wrote that Gröning had arrived in Bavaria, that Gröning was in Rosenheim, that Gröning was at the Traberhof. Seekers of healing immediately streamed together again. But there was no stopping them this time. All the dams broke. A real mass onslaught took place. Where once there had been 5,000 to 7,000 in Herford, there were now tens of thousands. Some days far more than 30,000 waited for Bruno Gröning at the Traberhof, wanting to see him, wanting him to heal them. The papers reported. The radio and weekly reviews sent their reporters. Even a movie was made, a film that documented the extraordinary events around the man from Danzig. It was shown in cinemas a few weeks later.

Dramatic scenes occurred, unbelievable things happened. One of the many newspapers that reported from the Traberhof was the Zeitungsblitz. In September 1949 it reported:

"More than 10,000 people have gathered there in the meantime, all of whom have been waiting for hours in the glowing heat for the great moment when Gröning stepped out onto the balcony, speaking to the crowd and radiating his healing energy.

The people stood tightly crowded together to get the full benefit of his 'healing rays'. Reactions soon began among the most severely ill in their wheelchairs and armchairs, or among individuals standing on the edge of the crowd.

Once again half-blind people began to see. Once again, people who had been handicapped began to raise themselves up. And once again paralyzed people began to move their stiff limbs. Hundreds reported increased pain in the diseased areas, as well as aches, stabbing and tingling, or sensing an

A film about Bruno Gröning was made at the Traberhof

indescribable 'light feeling' or of suddenly disappearing headaches."

A Host of Misery

A journalist who spent several days at theTraberhof described the scene from the balcony:

"As my eyes scan the crowd from the balcony, I believe I am seeing a true reflection of all of Germany's clinics and of all medical dictionaries spread out before me. I can see all types and stages of illnesses. The blind, lame, deaf, totally and partially paralyzed, amputees, people with TB and cancer, epileptics, babies and children, young women and women near the end of their lives, trembling old men and heavily made-up women."

Another journalist later wrote an entire book about the events at the Traberhof. He called it Die Grosse Umkehr

[The Great Turnaround]. He also described the host of misery that pressed around Bruno Gröning at the Traberhof:

"So many incurable illnesses and injuries, so much spiritual destruction or fear of life had been kept hidden inside houses, away from people's unsympathetic curiosity. Now all that became bitterly and inescapably visible. There were women and children with pale, careworn faces, with tortured, burning eyes that had already forgotten how to weep. There were amputees and paralyzed people, incapable of moving on their own. People shaken with cruel nervous cramps, with distorted faces covered in froth. Others were shaken with uncontrollable weeping. This is how they came together. This is how they were carried here. Thousands and thousands without end.

"Whatever powers for life and creativity, whatever happiness and confidence had ever been within them, it all lay trodden behind the barbed wire of prisoner-of-war camps, it

The host of misery

was buried under the ruins of their destroyed houses, it was left behind in their lost homeland.

"In those days and weeks I found nobody who had not been most deeply affected and shaken by this excess of suffering and misery, so terrible that it was beyond what anyone could ever have imagined. There was an immense number of pleading letters, in which all the people lamented their suffering who could not take the trip to Gröning for reasons of health or money. Whoever had a chance to see those letters would clearly see that the people who stood there for days, crowded together, awaiting their last hope, were just a small part of an endless crowd of sick, wounded and despairing people."

The Healings

It really was a host of misery crowding around Bruno Gröning. There were thousands of people whom nobody could help any more, who knew no way out of their suffering and misery. Something happened then that, according to the insights of modern science or worldly wisdom, couldn't really have happened, that shouldn't really have happened. But Bruno Gröning was not worldly and did not speak of science either. Bruno Gröning spoke of God, and the power of God worked. In the events at the Traberhof God showed Himself in all his glory and magnificence, in all His omnipotence, in all His strength and goodness. Numerous healings took place. Even when Bruno Gröning wasn't even there, the sick became healthy. One observer wrote thus:

"These were the days and nights before the great healing on September 9. Gröning himself was travelling in North Germany at the time when the first healings at a distance occurred among the sick. Under the overwhelming impression of such events, a slow change took place in the circle of the sick. Before their very eyes a force took effect for which there was no human explanation, and this power brought help where no human being had been able to help any more."

When Bruno Gröning then stepped onto the balcony and spoke to the people, scenes took place among the thousands of seekers of help that cannot be explained:

"Sick people stood up from their stretchers, lame people threw away their crutches and could walk, a blind child was able to see. Cries of gratitude announced new healings which could only partly be seen on the outside. Even two months later, and perhaps for a long time after that, healings continue to be made public as they happened or began in those days.

"From the terrace of the Traberhof one of our best doctors became an eye witness to this event. Deeply shaken, he confessed that as a result of those events he would take with him in his future life the faith that human beings were nothing without God's grace. And also that no knowledge or know-how could bring humans to healing if they did not show themselves to be humble and worthy of grace."

The Greatest Physician is our Lord God

In those days, just as in Herford, Bruno Gröning was not constantly at the Traberhof. He travelled a lot, apparently with the film team that was making the documentary film about him. So it was that those seeking healing sometimes had to wait for him for several days, which they did. One journalist described how Bruno Gröning then spoke to the waiting people:

"A few days later, when Bruno Gröning once more stood before the crowd of about eight or ten thousand people, he spoke briefly before leaving for Bremen. He asked the following questions:

"'Do you have patience?' – 'Yes!' from many voices, 'Do you trust me?' - Again, a roar of 'Yes!' 'Do you have and do you maintain your faith in the Lord God?' For the third time the chorus of Gröning's listeners answered 'Yes!'

"'So, I'll say goodbye to you in God's name!'

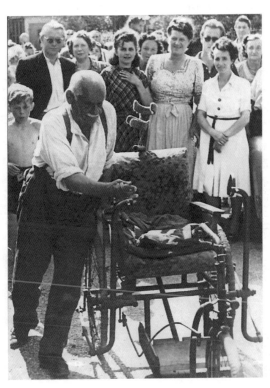

The lame walk

"Rising up to us on the veranda comes a shout from a man who had been struggling hard for air just a few minutes ago: 'I am healthy! I had asthma! I thank you, Gröning!'

"Then Bruno Gröning, the giver of healing, continues speaking.

" 'My dear ones! Don't think of your illness now. Put it behind you and concentrate just on that which you feel in your body! That is already happening which must happen for each individual, what they deserve and what they wish for themselves. Your heart, your body, your soul must be pure. Then God can enter, where until now Satan was, then I can help you all! In the end you are all God's children. But the greatest physician is and remains our Lord God!' "

Bruno Gröning speaking from the balcony at the Traberhof

The Same Thing Everywhere

Wherever Bruno Gröning appeared in 1949, in the shortest time, people by the dozen, the hundred and the thousand came streaming together. The name of Gröning electrified crowds of people and set them in motion. A journalist wrote about a Gröning visit in Munich in September 1949:

"Around 7 p.m. thousands of people stood in the Sonnenstraße. They were still standing there at 10:30 p.m. I had seen a lot during five years of war, but I was never more shaken than in the four hours during which I sat opposite Bruno Gröning and experienced a horrible parade of misery and suffering. Epileptics, the blind and the lame on crutches struggled towards him. Mothers held up their lame children to him. People fainted, screams were heard, supplicating cries for help, prayers, wishes."

Sick people on stretchers, the lame, the blind, the dumb, everywhere it was the same picture. Bruno Gröning was no pop star gathering fans around him. The poorest of the poor came to him, the sick, those who had been given up, the hopeless, those who didn't stand a chance any more and who could no longer be helped by anyone. He took them on, enlightened them, telling them that God is the supreme physician, that God could still help where people no longer could. Then a miraculous thing happened: sick people took in some hope, some faith, some power of faith, and many of them became healthy again. The sick stood up from their stretchers, the lame could walk again, the blind could see and the dumb could speak again.

A Contemporary Witness Reports

A woman who was at the Traberhof at that time reported what she experienced there:

"There were at least ten to twenty thousand people at the horse farm, but no Gröning in sight. So we waited for hours. The crowd of people was not hysterical. People there had faith and hoped to become healthy again. It was shocking to see these people lying on boards, or walking on crutches: crippled or lame people and war wounded. One could barely stand to look at them. But everyone had the same wish: 'I want to be healthy again!'

"Then Gröning arrived, went onto the balcony and spoke to the people through a microphone. He said that we should pay attention to our body, to see if we felt some tingling or flowing, as this meant healing. Then I felt an electric current, some vibrating, and a tingling through my entire body. Only then did I see how other people's bodies were trembling and shaking. It happened quite automatically, as though all their limbs were flying away. I would not have believed it if I had not seen it with my own eyes.

"Then people cried out, 'I don't need my stick any more!', 'I can see again!', and so forth. So I went through the crowd of people again, which was very difficult as we all stood tightly packed together, but I wanted to see what was going on and who had been crying out.

"All of a sudden some Red Cross attendants carried a paralyzed man along, lying on rough boards. He lifted his hands and with the help of the Red Cross attendants he slowly sat up. Sweat was running down him as he did so. When I asked him, he told me that he was a war veteran. Then he stood up.

"Then I saw a man crying. He had built a very primitive little wagon from some boards for his eight-year-old grandson. The boy could not walk and so he had been on the road with his grandson the whole day. I asked the man why he was crying and he told me that his grandson could walk now, but that he was afraid to go home, because when his daughter would see him she might get a heart attack.

Then I saw a smart-looking young Gypsy girl slide on her knees and I also spoke to her. She told me that she had always had such cramped-up hands, but that she could open them up now. She gave thanks again and again.

I saw so many who received their healing. One man jumped over the fence and I said to him, "Hey, you really are out of place here," to which he replied that five days ago he had still been walking on crutches. He showed me his wartime disability ID, which confirmed that he had been 100% paralyzed.

Carnival of the Press and Money Makers

In contrast to the negative attitude in Herford, the authorities in Bavaria held back. The provincial minister even made favorable comments about Bruno Gröning. He said that one should not permit such an extraordinary figure as Bruno Gröning to fail just because of the laws.

But the events at the Traberhof also had their dark sides. The more people gathered, the worse the conditions became. The press published huge special editions and kept reporting more aggressively, driven by greed for profit and the lust for sensation. They weren't interested in helping the sick or supporting Bruno Gröning. They only wanted to sell as many papers as possible by using the name of Gröning, and so make as much money as possible. To do this, some of them were even prepared to spread lies and invent stories about Bruno Gröning, making fun of him and dragging his name in the dirt.

Many money makers also came to the Traberhof. They did everything to make money from the misery of the people waiting there. Some sold photos of Bruno Gröning. Others sold seats for exhausted people, or food and drinks for the hungry. Others said that they knew Bruno Gröning or one of his helpers and could take the sick to him - for money, of course.

The conditions finally became impossible to stand. Bruno Gröning had come to the Traberhof to escape the commotion around him, but now everything was much worse than before. Wonderful mass healings that had never been seen before took place at the Traberhof, but the bad things going on around them became more and more threatening. Bruno Gröning had to leave the Traberhof.

The Traberhof was a world-famous event
Ten thousand people crowded there to Bruno Gröning

6. OUT OF THE FRYING PAN,
INTO THE FIRE

Ever since Herford it had been Bruno Gröning's greatest goal to build sanatoria, houses of healing in which he could work in orderly conditions and where the seekers of healing could receive healing undisturbed. As in Heidelberg, doctors were to do preliminary and follow-up examinations, check the healings and document the results.

Bruno Gröning received many offers to build such sanatoria. People came to him from everywhere, offering their help or putting houses at his disposal. But most of them unfortunately turned out only to be hoping for good profits. The houses were usually inns, hotels or guesthouses, with owners hoping for full houses and full cash boxes while taking advantage of the famous guest. Hardly anyone thought of the poor sick people or of Bruno Gröning.

A very special assistant who approached him at that time and later became his manager, was the business man Otto Meckelburg, from the North Sea island of Wangerooge. He had come to Bavaria with his wife to ask Bruno Gröning for help. His wife had been very ill, and they both followed Bruno Gröning everywhere, but kept arriving too late. Wherever they arrived, Bruno Gröning had already left. Nevertheless, Mrs. Meckelburg was healed even before she met Bruno Gröning in person. Out of gratitude, Meckelburg wanted to help Gröning and presented him with solid plans for building some sanatoria. Bruno Gröning listened to them, and at the end of December 1949 they both went to Wangerooge. Meckelburg organized many talks for Bruno Gröning there, on neighbouring islands as well as on the mainland. He spoke and once again innumerable healings occurred.

"You are healthy"

Antje Janssen was only five years old when she met Bruno Gröning on Wangeroode. Her mother had brought her because little Antje suffered from very bad skin ezcema, scratching her arms bloody and barely able to sleep. A talk had been announced at the local cinema that evening. Many people came. Antje Janssen remembers:

"The hall was full of people, tightly packed, with some people in wheelchairs as well, and some who had limped in on crutches. We sat on folding chairs and waited, but Bruno Gröning did not come. I fell asleep between my mother's knees.

"Mr. Gröning finally came after midnight. He said that the handicapped should join him on the stage, which they did, although you had to go up steps to get there. They laid aside their crutches and formed a circle around him.

"My mother was disappointed that she had not been called up onto the stage and simply went up with me. Everybody was horrified. I was ashamed and found it embarrassing when my mother pulled up my sleeves in front of Bruno Gröning, showing him my arms. No child would touch me then, it was so bad.

"To a child of five, Bruno Gröning seemed very tall. He bent down, swept through the air above my arms and said, 'You are healthy!' To my mother he said, 'Go home and let your doctor confirm that in fourteen days!'

"We went home then and I slept a whole day and night without scratching once. Today only the scars are still visible and I have been healthy to this day.

"There were some other healings. I heard from a boy in the children's home. He had previously been on crutches. Bruno Gröning had called from his window, 'Come on up to me!'

'But I can't with my crutches,' the boy had answered. But Bruno Gröning had called, 'Then throw them away!' The boy had thrown them away and walked through the corridor, through the hall and up the stairs to him."

Otto Meckelburg, the Money Maker

Bruno Gröning offered Otto Meckelburg his full trust and put himself totally at his disposal. He undertook to support him in everything, and to do whatever he could to help Meckelburg's plans to succeed. He also agreed to work exclusively with Otto Meckelburg and with no one else. A contract was drawn up between them, which specified that Bruno Gröning was only permitted to do what Meckelburg wanted.

In January Meckelburg founded the "Association for Research into Gröning's Healing Methods." He himself became the business manager, drawing a monthly salary of 1,000 Marks, which was a lot of money in those days. Bruno Gröning got nothing.

It soon became evident that Meckelburg did not care about what Bruno Gröning wanted and what goals he had. Even the sick people who still came in crowds to Bruno Gröning did not concern him. Meckelburg only saw a source of money in the "miracle worker" and made fun of him as "the best horse in his stable." He had bound Bruno Gröning to him with the contract, and Gröning had to do what he demanded. Meckelburg made a lot of money during that time, but he did not build the promised sanatoria. During a court trial later on he said, "I had no personal interest in the sanatoria."

Bruno Gröning with Otto Meckelburg

In June 1950 Bruno Gröning finally succeeded in freeing himself from Meckelburg, who was an ex-concentration camp commander. But by then Gröning's name had been ruined by his manager's dishonest practices. Meckelburg swore revenge, saying:

"I'll get that Groning down, I'll break all his bones."

The Swindle Revealed

Following the Meckelburg events, Bruno Gröning worked for a few months with a complementary health practitioner from Munich, Eugen Enderlin. Enderlin had received healing at the Traberhof and offered to let Bruno Gröning to give some talks at his home. Here, too, many healings took place, as Grete Häusler remembers,

"I too had read all kinds of good and wonderful things about Bruno Gröning in 1949. Yet I made some rather sneering remarks about him. What's more, I condemned him and his actions and called him hateful names, because I believed that it was all a trick.

"I would never have gone to him myself because I could not believe in anything "divine". But a friend of mine who was blind wanted to go to one of his talks. She needed an escort and could not find anyone else, so I had to help. I went to Munich with her and I wanted to go to the talk as well, to convince myself. I wanted to be able to tell my friend what a hoax it all was, so she could go and spend her money elsewhere.

"As I listened very sceptically to the introduction by Mr. Enderlin, I felt very uncomfortable that he asked us to pray quietly. I simply couldn't. I didn't believe in anything. I didn't believe that I could ever become healthy either.

"But I could and did follow the request to think of something beautiful. When I thought of beautiful Lake Wörther, which I had seen at sunrise the day before, a tingling sensation started in my toes. This tingling climbed high up to my neck and into my head. I felt some pain in my head, around my middle, and an ache in my arms down to my fingertips.

"At first I thought that someone must have secretly put up radiation lamps somewhere, but I could not find any in the room. I couldn't understand how one could feel something like that without having had an injection or some medication.

"Then Mr. Enderlin gave us a very good explanation about how for the Heilstrom*, the healing current, God was the great power station and Bruno Gröning was the transformer. Bruno Gröning wasn't even there yet. How was it supposed to work? Yet, whether I wanted to or not, I had to believe

---

* **Heilstrom:** see glossary of German words on page 6

that something was going on here that we humans no longer understand.

"Mr. Enderlin then said that it depended upon everyone individually whether they walked out the door healthy or not today. I listened very hard. I thought to myself, 'That wouldn't be bad at all, but there's no such thing!' No, there could be no such thing.

"I had had chronic suppurating frontal sinusitis for 15 years. How could it simply disappear? No! Or my destroyed liver cells? Or how could I have enough sugar in my blood again? That wouldn't be bad if it were that simple!

"But I thought about it again: 'Something about this whole story must be true, otherwise I would not have felt such pain and such aches in my body! Yes, walking out of here healthy today, that wouldn't be bad. But there is no such thing!'"

"The train brought you here!"

"When Mr. Gröning himself came, my pain became unbearably strong. I could hardly sit any more. After five minutes I instinctively knew that this man in front of me knew more and was able to do more than anybody else.

"After about an hour he came towards me and asked me, 'How did you get to Munich?' I answered, 'By train.'

'No, impossible, I cannot!' he replied. I could not see any connection. But I suddenly realized that his words were my own words. I had spoken them to my mother at home in Kärnten two weeks earlier as I had read my girlfriend's letter to her. 'No, impossible, I can't do it!' I was supposed to take my friend to Munich to see Gröning on August 28!

"I was horrified that Bruno Gröning knew everything I had told my mother, especially how I had criticized him. I realized that he didn't just know that. He knew everything about me and my life. I was unspeakably ashamed.

"He looked at me, lovingly, forgivingly. 'You didn't get here by train [Zug], but the pull [Zug] drew you here!' So I knew that he had forgiven me everything. Only much later did I understand his play on words, 'The train/pull brought you here'. I hadn't wanted to come to him, but I was allowed to come.

"Later Bruno Gröning stood in front of us, very serious and concentrated, and said, 'Give me your illnesses and your

Grete Häusler with Bruno Gröning

61

worries! You can't deal with them alone. I carry them for you. But you must give them to me of your own free will, I do not steal!'

"Again I started to feel so strange. Who was he, to be able to say such a thing? But I knew just one thing: I had not yet had such a request from anyone in my whole life, and I knew that I wouldn't meet anyone again in my whole life who would make me such an offer. So, at that very moment I had a unique opportunity in my whole life! And now I wanted to do it. But how? I didn't know how to give him my chronic frontal sinusitis, my damaged liver or my pancreas that produced too little sugar.

"I really didn't know how to do it. Since no other possible way was left to me, I did it like a child. I thought to myself, 'There you have them, my three incurable ailments. There you have my incurable mother. There you have it, all my unhappiness and everything that has gone topsy-turvy in my life. I don't want it any more!' At that very moment, I was rid of it all.

"The Einstellen* pain went on intensely. At the end of the talk Bruno Gröning told us that we should do Einstellen daily to receive the Heilstrom, the good energy, because everybody uses up energy through thinking, speaking and working. We should get this energy back through doing Einstellen, even when we are quite healthy, in order always to remain full of energy and health. But if someone is not quite healthy yet, it is all the more important to fill up completely with the good strength, because that will then drive out the evil. Finally, Bruno Gröning said goodbye."

---

* **Einstellen:** see glossary of German words on page 6

"Don't thank me, thank God instead!"

"We stayed a little while longer, because we wanted to ask him if we could come again. When the people had left the room and my friend and I were there alone, I noticed that I no longer had a headache. I had no aches, no tingling nor any pain any more, yes, I had nothing any more. I experienced such a wonderful light feeling, as light as if I had lost a ton of heaviness and fatigue. A feeling of happiness filled me more than I had ever known before. I said to my friend, 'Hey, Maria, I'm healthy!' She answered indignantly, 'You're crazy.' But I said, 'What I am feeling in my body right now can't be anything but good health.'

"Then Bruno Gröning came into the room. I ran towards him and shook his hand and said, 'I thank you, Mr. Gröning. I feel quite healthy now!' He looked me through and through, seeming very happy, and replied,

'Yes, you don't just feel it, you are. Don't thank me, thank God instead! He has done it.'"

Huge Sums Cashed In

Enderlin turned out to be a money maker as well. He was not interested in helping either, but he wanted to make as much money as possible by using Gröning. The fate of Bruno Gröning or of the sick didn't interest him at all.

Enderlin had promised to write an official document that was to prove that Bruno Gröning's work had nothing to do with the legally protected activity of complementary health practitioners. If that was so, then Bruno Gröning had not broken the law and so a healing ban against him was not justified. The path for Bruno Gröning to work freely was to be smoothed that way. He himself once wrote about that occasion:

"Mr. Enderlin did not keep this promise. But he took huge sums of money for himself and I did not get a single penny. That money allowed him to buy himself a villa in Feldafing and fill it with new furniture.

Towards the end of 1950 Bruno Gröning separated from Enderlin as well. In 1952 – 1953 a second try at cooperation with him failed for the same reasons. That time too Enderlin still had nothing but his own profit in mind.

He Puts up with Swindlers

People kept coming to Bruno Gröning and promising to help him with the development of his work. But many of them were only interested in making as much money as possible by using him. His former host, for instance, Mr. Hülsmann, the engineer from Herford, in time had also become an enthusiastic businessman.

Bruno Gröning seemed to attract such money makers, as light attracts moths. They kept crowding around him. They kept harming his reputation and his name. If they could not achieve their goals, or after they had parted from him, they tried to force him to pay them money or to harm him in any other way they could.

Why did Bruno Gröning keep letting such "helpers" get close to him? Why did he keep falling for them? Why didn't he simply keep them away?

During a talk in Munich on August 31, 1950, he explained why:

"What some people have not left untried up to now was to make some money from this little man with his knowledge

Bruno Gröning exposed the cheats

and know-how. They believed they had found a gold mine. In part they have had the possibility to make some money, but, thank God, it was no benefit to them.

Such people have to exist as well, because one must be able to determine who human beings are, that human beings can walk over dead bodies, not asking whether the sick are being helped or not. There are some people who will walk over dead bodies and just calmly see a sick person lying there. Those people never asked about the sick, they left nothing untried to be close to me.

I know the question pops up here and there, "Well, if this man knows so much, how come he did not know that? Maybe he doesn't know anything." Whether I do, and how much I do know, you'll get to know by and by. But this had to be. This material was needed for building up [the work], to free the path for all of you."

Bruno Gröning needed such people too, in order to free the path back to God. He wanted and had to uncover these unscrupulous bloodsuckers. He had to unmask them, so that people could see their dirty tricks. He had to tear the mask from the face of those heartless swindlers once and for all.

In the past, fine words had always been used by those money makers to trick their fellow humans and to hide their true intentions, covering up their selfish intentions. They always produced these fine words - "We just want to help,"- but they did evil deeds: exploiting suffering people and walking over dead bodies to make their own fortunes.

Bruno Gröning put an end to it. He allowed those people to get close to him and uncovered their shameful deeds. As they were parting on one occasion, Grete Häusler wished that he would never again be attacked by false helpers. He replied,

"Quite wrong, it must be so! I know what people carry inside them. But if I were to tell people: 'That one is a liar, that one is a swindler, a thief, nobody would believe me. What must I do? I have to draw those people to me, to teach them what is good, move them to turn their lives around and then give them a chance to lie, to swindle and to steal. If they still do it, everybody knows who they are. Then I let them come very close to me, and I'm not cowardly, then I fight."

Human beings can be free of this type of money maker in the future, and must no longer allow themselves to be blinded and tricked by their fine words. The evil tactics of such people can no longer be able to cut off humankind's connection to God. Bruno Gröning gave us that, but at a bitter price.

7. NEW PATHS

In 1949 the journalist Dr. Kurt Trampler came to the Traberhof as a reporter and, much to his own surprise, had experienced a great healing. Out of gratitude he wrote a book, Die Grosse Umkehr [The Great Turnaround], and committed himself to Bruno Gröning in other ways as well. He put him up in his house and organized lectures for him at the guesthouse Weikersheim in Gräfelfing near Munich in 1950 - 1951.

The Healings Continue

Just as with Enderlin, the talks in Gräfelfing were also well attended. Many healings took place. Anni, Baroness Ebner von Eschenbach, who later also became a good friend of Bruno Gröning, attended many of those talks and recorded some of her experiences with Bruno Gröning. Here is an extract:

"During his speech, things were happening in all corners and both ends of the room. People threw away their crutches and approached Gröning with radiantly happy faces, calling out, 'I can really walk freely again without a cane and with no pain!' They ran out of the room right away and went running up and down stairs. Their stiff limbs first had to get going again. Some of the men and women wanted to give their crutches to Gröning, but he said, 'I would have to bring my own removals van!' Gröning often broke canes that were as thick as a fist, as if they were matchsticks.

"Once a young woman with a very drawn face sat in the second row with a young girl of about nine. Gröning asked her, 'Well, Mummy, what do you feel?' She answered, 'Nothing, unfortunately, Mr. Gröning.'

"'Well, Mummy, don't keep looking back to the past! The terror of it is still stuck in you. You have to let go of it first. It was during a bombing raid. You were in a kind of garden shed and were buried while you were eight months pregnant. When you were rescued, the child came into the world and was blind. Is that right?' Amazed, the woman replied, 'Yes, exactly.'

"Bruno Gröning replied, 'Well now, don't think of that time of terror any more. Have firm faith in God's help and ask Him! You need not always bring the little child with you, so long as her Mummy has firm faith.'

"A week later the woman was back. The careworn look in her face was gone. She was literally rejuvenated. When Gröning asked her this time, she replied, 'Yes, today a warm feeling is trickling through me and I feel happy and free!' 'Now, Mummy, stay with it, it'll be ready to happen soon.'

"A week later the woman came again and in the middle of the lecture Bruno Gröning walked towards her, stood still and said, 'Mummy, on Thursday, at 5:20 p.m. you'll take your little child and lead her into a darkened room. She will see, but as she has never known colours or shapes, she would be scared and the fright might make her ill. Get her used to everything around her slowly.'"

"As I was particularly interested in that case, later on I made enquiries and found out that everything had happened to the minute, just as Bruno Gröning had predicted. A few years later I asked Bruno Gröning himself about the child once more and heard that her vision was normal, as though she had never been blind."

Trampler Becomes a Healer Himself

Bruno Gröning was attached to Kurt Trampler by a very special bond of friendship. But that connection broke as well. The time came when Trampler started to believe that he could heal by himself and did not need Bruno Gröning any more. He thought he had learnt enough from Gröning, so he left him and made himself independent as a healer. He even said, "Compared to me, Bruno Gröning is just a little orphan boy."

Trampler took the health practitioners' examination, set up as a healer and began publicly to say bad things about Bruno Gröning and to slander him.

Bruno Gröning did not do anything against Kurt Trampler and on his side kept up their special friendly relationship. In response to questions from confused seekers of healing as to whom they should now go to, Gröning or Trampler, he answered, "As long as people cannot yet have access to me, I will give him the power."

The First Big Trial

In 1949 the authorities in Bavaria had still been positive towards Bruno Gröning and the Bavarian Ministry of the Interior had even described his actions as a free act of charity. However, this positive attitude changed in 1950. Otto Meckelburg's schemes in particular had seriously damaged Bruno Gröning's reputation with the authorities. In September 1950 they issued a healing ban in Bavaria as well. Once again he was accused of having broken the Health Practitioners' Law and of having made people healthy, although he was not actually permitted to do so. A court case was even being prepared against him.

It took place in 1952. Bruno Gröning stood before the court. How humiliating that must have been for him. He had always done everything to help needy, suffering people, never thinking of himself, never asking the sick for money, and now he was being accused of doing exactly that. He was dragged before the judges because he had helped people.

In March 1952 the judgement was pronounced. Bruno Gröning was declared free. But the State Justice Department, which had prosecuted him, was not prepared to accept the judgement and appealed against it. In July there was another trial. Once more Bruno Gröning was declared innocent. That was good, but the reason was not. The judge said that Bruno Gröning had in fact broken the Health Practitioners' Law. However, he had been freed because he had not known he was breaking it and had done so without meaning to. But from that time on, Bruno Gröning was expected to be aware

Bruno Gröning before the judge

of this and not do it again. The acquittal was therefore like a new healing ban for Bruno Gröning.

The Healing Practitioners' Examination?

After the trial, Bruno Gröning continued his tireless search for ways to help the sick and to be able to carry out his mission, his calling, without getting into conflict with the law again.

He was even prepared to take the health practitioners' examination, even though he deeply detested dealing with illness or treating it, because he only saw evil in it. His work had nothing to do with treating illnesses. He only wanted to restore human beings' connection to God and open the path to health again for them.

In 1953 Bruno Gröning applied to take the health practitioners' exam in Stuttgart. But the application was refused for very questionable reasons. It seemed that every attempt was being made to suppress Bruno Gröning's activity under all circumstances and to deny him any possibility to work freely.

The "Gröning Pills"

In order to assist those seeking help, Bruno Gröning still aimed to build sanatoria. In 1953 he once wrote,

"My friends, countless calls for help reach me every day from all over the world. It is unfortunately impossible for me to follow them all up. A sanatorium must therefore be built in which I can work under orderly conditions. A lot of money has been offered to me for this, but I had to refuse it, as my work cannot tolerate any money makers. I can only accept help from people who are pure of heart."

The offer of a certain Rudolf Bachmann presented a good opportunity to collect the money for building sanatoria. Bachmann proposed building a "dynamic biological laboratory." In this laboratory he wanted to produce healing products under the direction and with the help of Bruno Gröning. Sick people from all over the world would have been able to

Bruno Gröning with the remedies G52 and L52

receive help that way and Bruno Gröning would have received the money he needed to build his sanatorium.

Bruno Gröning accepted the proposal and the products "G 52" and "L 52" were actually produced. They were tested at the university in Munich and received high approval. Bruno Gröning wrote about it,

"The Ministry of the Interior of the State of Bavaria issued the licence to produce these products. The pharmaceutical industry has great interest in these products: factories abroad want to take up the production and well-known companies in the Federal Republic of Germany had offered to buy certain formulas."

But it all turned out differently. Bachmann was a very keen businessman. Although Bruno Gröning wanted the products to be given only to pharmacies, Bachmann wanted to distribute them privately and sold them to friends from Bruno Gröning communities. Bruno Gröning could not agree to that. The friends in the communities were, after all, connected to him. They knew how to obtain and take in the healing power. They did not need those products. But Bachmann saw it as a simple way to doing some good business.

Rudolf Bachmann harmed Bruno Gröning very much by the way he acted. He needed a lot of money to build the laboratory and Bruno Gröning borrowed it from various friends for him. But Bachmann never built it the way Bruno Gröning wanted it. When Bachmann finally died, he left a debt of thousands of deutsch marks that Bruno Gröning had to pay. Instead of getting money to build a sanatorium, Bruno Gröning was now sitting on a huge pile of debts.

The Gröning Alliance

Bachmann, who was probably hoping for some better sales opportunities in the communities, suggested the foundation of the Gröning Alliance, and Bruno Gröning allowed it in 1953. These communities had already existed since the early fifties. Bruno Gröning had founded them to give his friends a chance to gather in his name to work with his teaching about faith. He visited the individual communities from time to time and gave talks on faith there.

The newly founded communities were to be grouped with-

Bruno Gröning speaking in a community hour

in the newly founded alliance. This was to give everybody a chance to find their way to health again. The alliance had set itself the task of making the path free for helpless people, assuring seekers of help that they could be healed as well.

The alliance was also intended to give Bruno Gröning legal protection for his work. Under the protection of the alliance he was to appear in public only as a speaker giving talks. In this way he would be protected by the basic law of freedom of speech. This was done to avoid any further conflict with the Health Practitioners' Law.

Some well-known and respected personalities were on the board of the Bruno Gröning Alliance, such as Count Zeppelin, Count Matuschka and Anny, Baroness Ebner von Eschenbach. Bruno Gröning became president for life.

Konstantin Weisser, a director, and Hermann Riedinger, a construction supervisor, assumed management of the business.

That all seemed very promising, as they were well-educated, and their worldly knowledge could benefit Bruno Gröning's work. But there was also the danger that they might raise themselves above him and act against his will. They were educated gentlemen, after all, while he was only a simple worker.

Egon Arthur Schmidt

The Heidelberg journalist and lecturer Egon Arthur Schmidt became secretary of the Bruno Gröning Alliance. He had already been his close collaborator in Herford, had written the book Die Wunderheilungen des Bruno Gröning [The Miracle Healings of Bruno Gröning] and founded the association "The Ring of Friends of Bruno Gröning."

But only a short time later that association had been dissolved again.

Bruno Gröning had separated himself from Schmidt in 1949 because he too had turned out to be a keen money maker. He had stolen donations and written negative newspaper articles. In one series of articles Schmidt, who was one of Gröning's closest collaborators at the time, described Bruno Gröning as a really bad person, very much harming his name in public, much as Meckelburg did later on.

In 1952 Schmidt once again turned to Bruno Gröning. He insisted that he had realized his mistakes and wanted to make up for everything. He asked to be allowed to help with the organization of the work. Although Bruno Gröning

Egon Arthur Schmidt in the mid-50s

knew Schmidt's motives, he took him on as his helper again. So once more Schmidt got a chance to show whether he was really concerned with the welfare of the sick or just his own financial advantage.

Unfortunately, it soon turned out that Schmidt had not changed. Again he tried to make some money from Gröning's ability. And again he harmed him with negative articles.

In 1955 Bruno Gröning finally left Schmidt, but after their separation Schmidt wanted to take revenge. He started several lawsuits against Bruno Gröning. He really wanted to squeeze as much money out of him as possible. Bruno Gröning once described him as the worst and most evil man. Schmidt was also one of those about whom Bruno Gröning had said, "These people had to be, to really find out how human beings are, that human beings can walk over dead bodies, not asking whether the sick are being helped or not."

"I Suddenly Stood Up"

In spite of all the unpleasantness that Bruno Gröning encountered at that time, in spite of all the opposition forces that wanted to suppress his work, more wonderful healings happened. Gisela Knollmann made this report:

"When our doctor found that I had a prolapsed disc in my spine, we did not shy away from any effort or cost, but it was all in vain. I could only lie in one position and only walk very little, bent over, really crooked. I was hardly able to work any more. It looked as if I would end up in a wheelchair.

"That is when Gröning came to me. He did nothing but preach. After a while, about half an hour, I thought to myself, 'What he is saying is really nice, but I can do that myself. That's not what he is here for. What is it all about?'

"Very suddenly, in the middle of a sentence, he moved forward a bit, smacked my little side table with his hand and said, 'Well, I don't have any more time. I have to leave.'

"At that very moment, at that single moment, it happened.

"I cannot tell you what, I cannot explain it to you, not to this day, not after 45 years. I have no explanation, neither does my husband. In that one second he stood up and I stood up, as well.

I suddenly stood up and had no more pain. I could stand straight, really straight, the way I had grown naturally, the way I hadn't been able to stand any more for a whole year. I have had no more disc problems since then, for 45 years by now. I can walk without any complaints, without any handicap."

"It Was a Deliverance"

Adolf Groth was also very ill when he first met Bruno Gröning. He had stomach cancer and had already been given up by the doctors. Many years later he reported during a newspaper interview:

"The war had marked us, the war had destroyed us. That was the whole thing. Spiritually broken. We were not normal people during the war. We really were hyenas. As a normal human being, you can't shoot someone, but then we had to. It was you or me. That's just not normal.

"Life hung by a straw and so you kept looking for something. Just like when you are on the front, you look for a straw to hang on to. At any moment it can all be over.

"It is terrible when you experience something like that. So it's no wonder that we got sick, that we were destroyed spiritually. I was so sick, I had one foot in the grave. I wanted help. I couldn't eat anything or do anything any more. As I found out later, my family doctor had said that I had stomach cancer.

"Then we drove over there. I don't know exactly how it came to be any more, but anyway there were several of us people. So we drove there and then there was a deliverance. It was deliverance for us, for everybody who had been there. The hall was filled. It was deliverance for all of us. It was as if we were new-born.

One felt so light, the heaviness had come out of the body. And at that moment and also as we drove away, we were no longer ill. We felt nothing more of the illness. It was gone.

As soon as I got home, I could eat again and the illness did not come back either. So simple! But this was the transfer of Bruno Gröning's energy, which he had radiated. The body was charged and then the body's circulation was freed again, flowing and energized. I'll put it this way, everything could work normally again. But whoever doesn't want to believe it, has to let it be. But as for my faith, no one can take it from me."

8. THE GREAT TRIAL

In spite of all the wonderful reports, there were still forces at work that wanted to destroy Bruno Gröning by any means. In March 1955 he was accused again of having broken the Health Practitioners' Law.

But this time there was a second accusation. Bruno Gröning was accused of negligent homicide, or manslaughter. The prosecution lawyer alleged that Bruno Gröning had promised healing to 17-year-old Ruth Kuhfuß and prevented her from going to a doctor in 1949. She had died at the end of 1950 because she had no longer wanted to be treated by a doctor.

A Serious Accusation

That was a really serious accusation. Had Bruno Gröning truly been responsible for the death of that girl? The newspapers ran the story with big headlines. The public became agitated. For many people, Gröning's guilt was determined in advance.

He himself wrote a letter to his friends a few days after the accusation. He replied to the accusations in a statement.

"I am supposed to have promised healing to a 17-year-old girl suffering from TB at the end of 1949 and prevented her from seeing a doctor or going to a sanatorium. I am said to be responsible for the death of that young human child. (…)

Of course, things are very different from the way they are being presented. I don't need to explain it to my friends.

Bruno Gröning – accused in the great trial

They know that I don't make any "promises of healing" and that I never advise against medical treatment.

I was acquitted in 1952. Is it not peculiar that, although all the documents were already at hand, the 'Kuhfuß case' that had occurred in 1949 - 1950 was not pursued at the time of the trial against me in 1951 - 1952?!

Is it not strange that procedures for a new trial against me were begun exactly when the public found out that the 'Gröning Alliance' was started in Murnau on November 22. 1953? Since 1954 many local community leaders and friends as well as alliance members have been questioned and kept under surveillance."

The Kuhfuß Case

Among the witnesses for the prosecution were two former collaborators of Gröning: Eugen Enderlin and Otto Meckelburg. Both did everything they could to harm Bruno Gröning and if possible to get him behind bars.

It was Enderlin who had laid the blame for the Kuhfuß case on Bruno Gröning. Immediately after the failure of their second collaboration in 1953, he had gone to the police and informed them of the events concerning Ruth Kuhfuß. Only then did the investigation begin.

But Meckelburg also played a decisive role in the Kuhfuß case and used this opportunity to make good on his threat, "I'll get Gröning down all right. I'll break all his bones."

The events around Ruth Kuhfuß had happened exactly during the time when Meckelburg was Bruno Gröning's manager: in Wiessee in November 1949 and in Säckingen in May 1950.

At the time Ruth Kuhfuß suffered from bilateral tuber-culosis of the lungs. Doctors had tried everything but they were not able to help, and after many painful treatments, the girl didn't want anything more to do with them. Her father, a savings bank employee, drove to Wiessee with her to a lec-ture of Bruno Gröning on November 5, 1949. When Bruno Gröning saw the girl for the first time, he knew right away that there was no more hope for her. He also mentioned it to one of the doctors present. But Meckelburg pressed him hard and demanded that he heal the girl. As a sly money maker, he hoped for a good source of income from the fa-ther. So he convinced him that Bruno Gröning could heal his daughter.

This led to a personal meeting between Bruno Gröning and Ruth Kuhfuß after the talk. Gröning gave the sick girl courage and asked her father to arrange for a medical specialist to examine her nine days later. He wanted to try and get the girl to take medical treatment again. Her father promised to take care of it.

Bruno Gröning didn't hear any more from Ruth Kuhfuß for a long time afterwards. It was only in May 1950 that Meckelburg told him that he wanted to drive him to the Kuhfuß family in Säckingen. In the meantime the father had sent some imploring letters to Gröning, asking for a visit.

Meckelburg had not passed the letters on to Bruno Gröning, but arranged for a meeting with Mr. Kuhfuß with-out Bruno Gröning's knowledge.

Bruno Gröning was very upset about Meckelburg's action. He did not want to visit the Kuhfuß family. It was clear to him that he could not help the girl any more. He had also thought that she was under medical treatment again. But Meckelburg forced him to come along. He smelled a good source of money in Mr Kuhfuß, who worked in a savings bank. He wanted to take advantage of him, but for that he needed Gröning. He also hoped to make some publicity with the girl's healing.

Later Meckelburg stated that Bruno Gröning had promised healing to Ruth Kuhfuß. But it was Meckelburg himself who had assured the father that he would make Gröning heal his daughter.

The main accusation brought against Gröning this time was that he had forbidden Ruth Kuhfuß to seek medical treatment. But against this was the fact that he had already sent the girl back to a doctor during their first meeting. (This was confirmed even by the witnesses for the prosecution.) During a speech on the radio in the fall of 1949, he had urged people "to go for follow-up medical checks afterwards." He kept advising seekers of help to trust their doctors.

Ruth Kuhfuß had already endured many painful, unsuccessful treatments. She refused to undergo any more. She died from her illness on December 30, 1950.

The First Trial

The preparations for the trial lasted over two years. Bruno Gröning's defense was made very difficult. Nearly all the witnesses who could have cleared him of guilt were rejected, but the witnesses for the prosecution were admitted.

Bruno Gröning could not grasp with how much malice and ill will they were proceeding against him. During one hearing, he once said:

"Should it be punishable if I show people the way how they can become healthy again and find the right path to do it? Thousands who are said to be incurable could become healthy if they knew about it. I do no more, after all, than make people aware that it depends totally upon their will whether they become healthy again, and I show them what they have to do to recreate order inside themselves. It has been proven a thousand times that people who followed my advice became happy again in their life. (...) After all, I don't harm anyone with my activities. On the contrary, I help everywhere that help was abandoned."

The trial began in Munich at the end of July 1957. After three days the judge passed judgement, acquitting him of the accusation of negligent homicide, but imposing a fine of 2,000 deutsch marks for breaking the Health Practitioners' Law.

At first sight the judgement seemed very positive. Acquitted on the most important point, negligent homicide, and the 2,000 mark fine could be got over. But for Bruno Gröning the judgement was unacceptable. It was equal to a final ban on his work.

But his lawyer made a mistake, so instead of Bruno Gröning appealing against the judgement, it was the State Justice Department that did so. It demanded that the whole case be reopened once more.

The second trial began again in Munich in mid-January 1958.

Separation From the Gröning Alliance

First, though, some decisive events took place within the Gröning Alliance. In October 1957 there was a serious dispute between Bruno Gröning and the management of the alliance. Although he was the president of the alliance, as time went on the men on the board had found it harder and harder to let Bruno Gröning tell them anything. They seemed to have forgotten that the alliance did not just bear Gröning's name, but also existed for his sake. The Gröning alliance developed a life of its own. They completely lost sight of the real goals, that of helping suffering people, and keeping Bruno Gröning free of burdens.

In a 62-page "statement about the activity of the alliance," Bruno Gröning dealt with all the points where the alliance had harmed him. He summed it up this way:

"Nowadays, when I compare my earlier companions (the money makers Meckelburg, Enderlin, Schmidt and Hülsmann) with my present companions (the members of the alliance board), I come to the same final result. Today the final outcome is that the same has happened as back then. Today, through those who want to be my greatest, closest and best friends, nothing different has come about to then. Then sordid businessmen swindled me. Today friends have failed me, because they could calmly watch me going through trials, through sentencing, because I received no help, that I could not visit my communities without a car, that they did nothing to stop the smear campaign by the press. These friends only created confusion because they simply were not there for me when I needed people who, with their education and position in worldly life, could and should have supported me, [and so] in the end it could not come to the work for which I am here on Earth.

"None of these friends committed their Ego to fighting for my freedom, none of them had the courage really to step in for me. Nothing happened. Like petty bureaucrats they just took decision after decision. Nobody really stepped in for me, nobody really threw everything into a total effort, so that they took off me all these struggles during the law suits, or against the press, or for helpers, for the car that had broken down, or against all the smut and slander, etc., etc. Nobody stood in front of me so that I could do what I am

The healing ban always dogged him after Herford

here on this Earth to do: to pass on to people the power of life and guide them to faith.

"That I need calm to do this and that I cannot be hampered again and again by worldly, superficial influences, that I need a real protective wall in order to let that take effect which was given to me: no one thought about that, none of my friends, or those who want to be my friends. And this is what is so shameful and such a disappointment for me:

- The moneymakers wanted to make their profit. They are recognized to be bad people.
- Friends from the Gröning Alliance are too tepid, too indifferent, too comfortable. I don't want to say illwilled.

Bruno Gröning in despair and
let down by his own friends

"But the outcome is the same: I was not set free. Many friends from the board of the alliance did not keep their promise. I was simply gagged by all these measures."

Bruno Gröning decided to break up the Gröning Alliance. The "Association for Furthering Psycho-Spiritual and Natural Life Principles" was founded in 1950 and the name of Bruno Gröning was not even mentioned in its statutes any more. Even this last association founded in Bruno Gröning's lifetime was not to achieve what he had hoped for.

His Word Bans Sickness

Bruno Gröning's work continued all during these discussions and struggles. In 1957 Dr. Horst Mann reported in a series of articles in the magazine Das neue Blatt under the title: "His Word Bans Sickness".

"The next morning I drove from Hameln to Springe, the little town on the Deister. A Gröning community had sprung up here as well. The healing of several people had been the starting point for it. As in various places in Schleswig-Holstei, in Augsburg, Hameln, Vienna, Plochingen and other towns, I experienced here too how people stood up and told me about their illnesses. They named the doctors who had treated them. They told me how they had regained their health and that they thanked Gröning for it. They were always prepared to raise one hand and confirm their statement under oath.

"As a baby, both my legs were already dislocated from their hip sockets," fifty-year-old Julie Prohnert from Hanover told me. "Later I could only walk with crutches. Our doctor could only relieve my suffering. As I listened to a talk by Mr. Gröning, I felt a strong reaction. My back, that was totally crooked by then, became straight again. I could walk again. I had no more relapses…"

"I had rheumatoid arthritis and was constantly plagued by rashes and abscesses. Mr. Gröning freed me from them," said Wilhelm Gabbert from Hameln.

"Only morphine could make the pain in my gallbladder bearable any more," reported Kurt Severit from Evestorf. "I thank Bruno Gröning for freeing me from this suffering."

"I had severe diabetes," reported Robert Thies from Springe. But even more threatening was the weakness of his heart muscle. "Neither ailment bothers me any more today. I thank Mr. Gröning for that."

"This list could go on. There were people of every age who gave me reports, men, women and children. Many illnesses were listed, from headaches through inflammation of the nerves, sciatica, kidney and gallbladder ailments to heart problems and paralytic symptoms.

"But there was something else that touched me profoundly. Many people freely told me here in front of everyone that they had experienced a great inner change through Gröning. Pursuing success and selfish attitudes had given way to calm and relaxation and communal thinking.

"During all these conversations with people who felt healed through Bruno Gröning, one question became stronger within me: 'Did everybody have success in receiving healing?' Or more specifically, 'Was it possible with every illness? Where were the limits of that power going out from Bruno Gröning? Were any dangers lurking there?' […]

"During my last visit I put that question to him. 'I can and will not force anybody,' he answered me. 'If someone closes himself up and has no willingness to develop the power to create order, then I lack the readiness to step in. I only ask those people to burst the lock of evil that is hindering healing.'

I had another question: 'Every illness is dangerous in a different way,' I said. 'Let's say a severely ill person has been given up by several doctors, but he gets a doctor who is still fighting for his patient to call you. Will you be able to help?'

"'Yes,' Gröning said. He said it without hesitation. 'If the patient believes it and the doctor trusts his own path, success will not fail to appear. The mutual trust will develop unsuspected forces in the patient. Success has often come most promptly when, full of despair, the sick person grasped at the last straw.'"

The Trial Continues

In January 1958 a new trial began again in Munich. It was to Bruno Gröning's great disadvantage that the State Justice Department had appealed, instead of him. But it was not just his first lawyer's negligence that harmed him. In the meantime Bruno Gröning had got a new lawyer and the first one took some time to hand over the trial file. By doing so, he hampered the preparation for the new lawyer decisively.

The prosecution witnesses gave evidence much more confidently this time than during the first trial. In the Kuhfuß case they seemed to have come to a mutual agreement on the point of "preventing the patient from seeking a physician".

This time the sentence was eight months' prison for negligent homicide and a fine of 5,000 deutsch marks for breaking the Healing Practitioners' Law. The sentence was commuted to probation. That meant that Bruno Gröning wouldn't have to go to jail, but he would have to prove his good behaviour for several years. If he did not commit any

Bruno Gröning in the dock

offense during that time, the prison sentence would not be carried out. But it didn't get that far. Bruno Gröning could not accept the sentence and his lawyer requested a revision of the case. Everything had to be worked through again.

Anny, Baroness Ebner von Eschenbach, who had attended both the trial in July 1957 and also the one in January 1958, described the judgement as a disgrace for Germany.

Bruno Gröning was very disappointed and upset. He complained bitterly that he was being punished for doing good. He was also hurt that during the entire trial nobody, not even his lawyers, had shown any serious interest in finding out how a healing came about. If they had cleared up that question, they would have understood that his work had nothing to do with the Health Practitioners' Law. The case would have been dismissed. But nobody at court was interested in it. They had already formed their opinion of Gröning and were not prepared to give it up.

The date for the appeal was set for January 22, 1959. But in the meantime something tragic happened in Bruno Gröning's life.

9. GOING HOME AND NEW BEGINNINGS

In November 1958, with his second wife Josette, a French woman whom he had married in 1955, Bruno Gröning drove to Paris for an examination by a doctor friend of his, Dr. Pierre Grobon. The findings of several X-rays showed that he was suffering from advanced cancer of the stomach. Dr. Gabon wanted to operate right away, but Bruno Gröning refused.

He drove back to Germany, because he still had something important to prepare for the communities. Then he drove back to Paris afterwards.

His Path Ends in Paris

In the meantime Dr. Grobon had informed a famous specialist, Dr. Bellanger. On December 8 Bruno Gröning underwent an operation at the clinic in the Rue Henner. The results were terrifying for the doctors. It was much worse than the X-rays had revealed. There was nothing that they do. The wound was closed immediately.

To his doctors' amazement, Bruno Gröning recovered very rapidly and drove back to Germany.

On December 26 he called a few of his closest friends together and gave a talk. None of them knew how unwell he was. He didn't let anyone notice anything.

In mid-January 1959 he met for three days with the board members of the new association, deciding how his work was to be developed further. None of them suspected that it would be their last meeting with him.

On January 21 he flew back to Paris. On the twenty-second he underwent another operation. At 9:00 a.m., at the

Bruno Gröning with his doctors

very hour the appeals proceedings began in Munich, Bruno Gröning was lying on the operation table in Paris. He had to endure what he had spared so many people. He neither could nor might help himself.

As he was lying under anaesthesia that morning, a severe storm suddenly broke over Paris with lightning and claps of thunder, and black clouds darkened the brightness of the day. It got so dark that the lights had to be put on. The nurse was very amazed at such a severe thunderstorm.

In the days following the operation, Bruno Gröning got up twice more and sat in an armchair. But on January 25 he fell into a coma, and on the following day, on January 26, 1959, at 1:46 p.m. Bruno Gröning died in the Henner Clinic in Paris.

Burnt Up Inside

The doctors indicated cancer as the cause of death, but after the second operation Dr. Bellanger also said,

"The destruction in Bruno's body is terrible. He is totally burnt up inside. It is a mystery to me how he could go on living like that without suffering the most frightful pain."

It came about the way Bruno Gröning had foretold it:

'If they forbid me to work, I'll burn up inside."

The healing ban that kept dogging him, the never-ending trial, the ongoing malice and spitefulness of his former collaborators, as well as the narrow-mindedness of his own friends, all this contributed to the fact that the man who had saved innumerable people from their pain and suffering, who had brought healing to thousands upon thousands of seekers of help, had to die so bitterly in Paris. Quietly and alone, none of his friends knowing about it, he bore all the suffering of humankind.

But even in death Bruno Gröning showed greatness. In December 1974, Dr. Bellanger wrote in a letter:

"Bruno Gröning was a man with a heart, a valuable man who prevailed. His dignity in the face of suffering and death causes amazement to this day."

Bruno Gröning's body was cremated in Paris and the urn was buried in the Waldfriedhof cemetery in Dillenburg.

The trial was declared closed and the final judgement was never given. Yet after the trial of January 22, Bruno Gröning's lawyer had expected that the sentence of January 1958 would be repealed.

Why did it all have to happen that way? Why did Bruno Gröning's path have to end like that? Why could he not help himself? During his talk to his closest friends on December 26, 1958, one month before he died, he said, "I have only one path to go, not a rose-covered one, a thorny path. But this path is so buried, so blocked, I have to clear it. I will clear it and when I have cleared it, it will always become blocked again."

In order to finally clear the path, so that every human being could regain his connection to God, so that everybody could have healthy, peaceful lives again, Bruno Gröning had to walk even the final stretch of his thorny path. It had to happen like that. It was not possible to help humankind any other way.

It was the final stretch on the path of a life that had not been easy, a life that had been totally for the service of God and of suffering humankind, a life that had demanded everything from him in love and service. Once he had rightly said: "My finest day on earth will be when I am allowed to go home to the glory of God."

But how could it go on now? Wasn't everything over now with Bruno Gröning's passing?

It Has Only Just Begun

When the news spread that Bruno Gröning had died, his friends scattered very quickly. A few remained, just a handful of faithful, but they experienced something that may be even more wonderful than what had happened during Bruno Gröning's life time: the healings kept happening. It came about as he had foretold:

"Everybody has to die, me too. They will lay my body in the earth, but I shall not be dead. I will be there for those who call me and I'll go on helping. But then everybody will experience help and healing from themselves."

Grete Häusler once told how she experienced the first healing after Bruno Gröning's passing:

"I shall never forget the first healing. I was in Duisburg at the time, right in the Ruhr district, on the third floor. I had had my third child and was lucky to have a cleaning lady at the time. The woman had been blind in one eye for fourteen years. Six specialists had told her that she would never be able to see out of that eye again. As she was dusting one day, Bruno Gröning's picture fell down and broke. She called me and as I saw the broken shards, the thought came to me, "I'll tell her now," and I asked her:

"Do you know who that is?"

"No," she said, "I don't know."

"That is Bruno Gröning," I said. "And it was through him that I experienced healing.'

She just looked at the picture and said, "What's going on? I feel something like an electric current running through my body from head to foot."

In that instant she received the healing energy for the first time and then I told her about Bruno Gröning and how I had experienced him.

A few days later she came again and told me, "Mrs. Häusler, I can see! This morning I was able to wipe some pus from my eye and since then I can see everything."

We were so moved. She took the picture book. She could read large script, small script. She could see the farthest distance from the window. That was the first great healing after Bruno Gröning's passing.

Many decades have gone by since. There are now Bruno Gröning friends all over the world. Healings are happening everywhere and Bruno Gröning's words keep coming truer and truer.

"My answer to all my opponents who must hate me:

What my opponents had to do, they have done completely and with that they are at an end. Even so I have done what I had to do but this is only the beginning."

"Whoever will call me, for them I shall be there,
and I go on helping."
Bruno Gröning